D0821257

Fun and Festive WINTER CRAFTS

Fun and Festive Crafts for the Seasons

Snow Globes, Groundhog Puppets, and Fairy Masks

Randel McGee

Enslow Elementary

an imprint of

Enslow Publishers, Inc.

40 Industrial Road
Box 398
Berkeley Heights, NJ 07922
USA

www.enslow.com

For my brothers Gary, Ken, and Steven!

Enslow Elementary, an imprint of Enslow Publishers, Inc.

Enslow Elementary® is a registered trademark of Enslow Publishers, Inc.

Library of Congress Cataloging-in-Publication Data

McGee, Randel.
    Fun and festive winter crafts : snow globes, groundhog puppets, and fairy masks / Randel McGee.
        pages cm.—(Fun and festive crafts for the seasons)
    Includes bibliographical references and index.
    Summary: "Includes the scientific explanation behind the winter season, a related myth, and step-by-step
        instructions on how to make eight winter-themed crafts out of various materials"— Provided by publisher.
    Audience: Ages 8-up.
    Audience: Grades 4 to 6.
    ISBN 978-0-7660-4317-6—ISBN 978-1-4644-0579-2 (pbk.)—ISBN 978-1-4645-1279-7 (epub)—
        ISBN 978-1-4646-1279-4 (single-user PDF)—ISBN 978-0-7660-5911-5 (multi-user PDF)
    1. Handicraft—Juvenile literature. 2. Winter—Juvenile literature. I. Title.
TT160.M385 2015
745.5—dc23

2013022080

Future editions:
Paperback ISBN: 978-1-4644-0579-2
Single-User PDF ISBN: 978-1-4646-1279-4

EPUB ISBN: 978-1-4645-1279-7
Multi-User PDF ISBN: 978-0-7660-5911-5

Printed in the United States of America

052014 Lake Book Manufacturing, Inc., Melrose Park, IL

10 9 8 7 6 5 4 3 2 1

Photo Credits: Crafts prepared by Randel McGee and p. 48; craft photography by Enslow Publishers, Inc.; Designua/Shutterstock.com, p. 5.

Cover photo: Crafts prepared by Randel McGee; photography by Enslow Publishers, Inc.

Contents

AUTHOR'S NOTE: The projects in this book were created for this particular season. However, I invite readers to be imaginative and find new ways to use the ideas in this book to create different projects of their own. Please feel free to share pictures of your work with me through www.mcgeeproductions.com. Happy crafting!

WINTER!

The Abenaki are an American Indian people from the northeast region of North America. They tell this story about how the seasons came about:

Long ago there lived a clever and brave hero named Glooscap. It became very cold in the land of the Abenaki. The fires could not give enough warmth, and the crops no longer grew. The people were hungry. Glooscap traveled to the North and found a wigwam made of ice and snow. Inside was the great giant Winter, whose icy breath caused the awful cold. Glooscap could not make Winter stop the Abenaki's suffering.

A bird told Glooscap that far to the South, the fair maiden Summer lived. Summer was the source of all warmth and beauty. Glooscap knew he had to have her help to break Winter's hold on the land. He rode on the back of a whale down the coast to the land where Summer lived and took her back to the home of Winter.

Summer's warmth and beauty softened Winter's frozen heart and melted his icy home. Winter agreed that he would not be as cold and would come only part of the year. Summer also agreed that she would visit Glooscap's people for part of the year so that their crops would grow and they could prepare for the cold days of Winter. The agreement still stands today.

This is a wonderful legend, but the cause of winter has more to do with tilting planets than frosty giants. Earth is tilted slightly from north to south. The top half of the planet is called the Northern Hemisphere (*hemi* means "half" and *sphere* means "ball"). As Earth revolves around the sun during the year, the Northern Hemisphere slowly angles away from the sun.

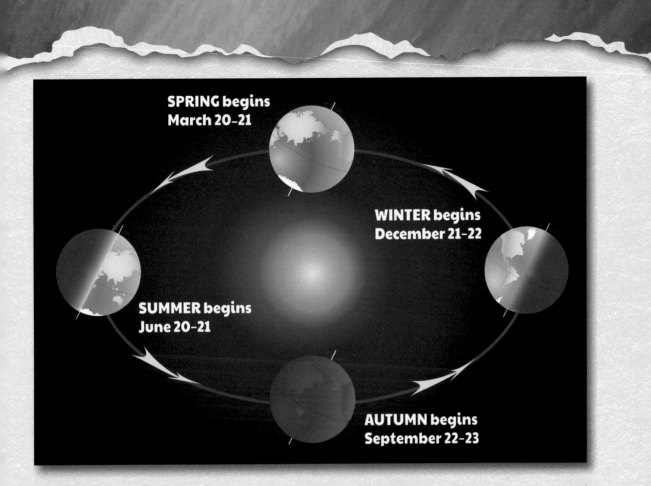

SPRING begins
March 20-21

WINTER begins
December 21-22

SUMMER begins
June 20-21

AUTUMN begins
September 22-23

This means the north gets less light and heat from the sun. For half the year, the minutes of daylight get shorter and less heat reaches the ground to warm it. On December 21, the Northern Hemisphere tilts farthest from the sun. This is the winter solstice, the first day of winter and the shortest day of sunlight.

Winter in the Northern Hemisphere officially arrives in December and continues until March. Snow and ice are found in many places. Nature seems to sleep. Yet it is a busy time for many people around the world as they celebrate special holidays such as Christmas and Hanukkah. Winter is also a time to enjoy such activities as building snowmen, ice-skating outdoors, sledding, and skiing.

So while you are inside on a cold winter's day, you can keep busy and entertain your family and friends with these fun and festive winter crafts!

WINTER WONDERLAND SNOW GLOBE

In the cold days of winter, snow often covers the land with a fluffy, sparkling blanket of white. It can be fun to watch the snowflakes dance through the air as they float to the ground. Snow globes have been a popular winter decoration for about two hundred years. You can make your own snow globe and watch the snow fly while staying snug and warm inside. *Ask an adult to help you.

WHAT YOU WILL NEED:

- a small glass jar with a watertight lid (baby food jars, jelly jars, olive jars, etc.) *Be sure to get permission whenever you use a recycled jar.

- waterproof glue

- small toys, figures, and trees of plastic or ceramic (Note: Do NOT use metal figures, as they may rust.)

- distilled water

- glycerin (found in drugstores)

- white or silver glitter

- air-drying clay

- acrylic paints and paintbrushes

#1

WHAT TO DO:

1. Thoroughly clean the small glass jar, inside and out, with warm, soapy water and remove the label and any glue with an adult's help.

2. Glue the toys, figures, and trees securely on the inside of the lid. Make sure that the figures will still fit inside the jar easily. Let the glue dry.

#2

3. Over a sink or basin, fill the jar to the top with distilled water.

4. **Ask an adult** to add three or four drops of glycerin to the water in the jar. Glycerin will slow the glittery snowflakes a little as they fall.

5. Add a few pinches of glitter to the water in the jar and let them settle to the bottom.

#5

6. Carefully put the lid, with the figures glued on securely, in place and screw it tightly to the jar. Some water will spill over into the sink or basin.

7. Sculpt a base for the snow globe from air-drying clay and let it harden.

#7

#8

8. Paint the snow globe base with acrylic paints or add other little decorations. You may glue the snow globe to the base or leave it loose as you wish. Shake the globe gently to start the "snowfall."

SNOWMAN PUPPET

If it snows enough in your yard, you can roll the snow into big balls and stack them up to make a snowman. You can decorate him with sticks for arms, rocks and buttons for a face, and an old knit cap on his head. But wait! Here is a snowman you can make inside that won't melt! Come up with a name and funny stories for this snowman.

WHAT YOU WILL NEED:

- two Styrofoam™ balls—one slightly larger than the other
- knife (*Ask a responsible adult to help.)
- felt or cloth scraps—pink and white
- black marker
- scissors
- white glue

- a paint stir stick (found in hardware stores)
- a 12-inch wooden dowel, ¼ inch in diameter
- small pebbles or buttons
- small twigs or pipe cleaners
- a small old or unmatched sock (*Be sure to get adult permission before using a sock.)

WHAT TO DO:

#1

1. **With adult supervision**, use a knife to cut the smaller Styrofoam ball in half. Trim off a bit from the side edge of one of the halves.

#2

2. Use the other half of the small Styrofoam ball to trace a circle on the pink felt or fabric. Cut out the circle.

#3

3. Fold the pink fabric in half and glue the two Styrofoam halves to it. Let the glue dry.

#4

4. Use the knife to make a slit in the rounded side of one half. Make sure it is parallel to the trimmed edge.

5. Put glue in the slit of the trimmed Styrofoam half and fasten it to the top of the paint stick. Let it dry.

6. Cut the larger Styrofoam ball in half and glue both halves to the paint stick to form the body of the snowman. Let the glue dry.

7. (a) Glue a strip of white felt or fabric to one end of the dowel with about an inch of fabric extending beyond the dowel. (b) When it is dry, glue the loose flap of fabric to the top and back of the puppet's head and let that dry. This rod will make the puppet's mouth open and close when you gently pull and push it.

#7b

8. Decorate the snowman with pebbles, buttons, twigs, or pipe cleaners. Use the toe of an old sock as a cap and scraps of the sock as a scarf for the snowman to wear.

#8

JACK FROST OR SNOW FAIRY MASK

In the cold of winter, strange designs of frost and ice appear on windowpanes and water puddles. Icy, glittery formations stretch down from rooftops, telephone lines, and tree branches. Vikings blamed an elflike character for creating ice and snow with his freezing power. Today we call that fellow Jack Frost. Stories about Jack Frost often include snow fairies who dance and play with him in the snow. You can pretend to be old Jack Frost or a dancing snow fairy with these masks.

WHAT YOU WILL NEED:

* scissors

* white poster board or sheet of craft foam— 12 inches x 18 inches

* pencil or permanent markers

* white glue

* two clothespins

* glitter glue—silver and blue

* yarn

WHAT TO DO:

1. Follow the instructions to get the pattern for the mask you want (see pages 41 and 42).

2. Fold the poster board or craft foam sheet in half.

3. Place the long dashed line along the fold of the craft foam or poster board. Trace the pattern with a pencil or marker.

4. Cut out the pattern on the solid black lines.

#1

#5

5. Fold the mask along the two short dashed lines of the pattern. Put a few small drops of glue on the inside of the fold and clamp it together with the clothespins on the outside of the fold. Let the glue dry, then remove the clothespins. This will give the mask more strength.

6. Decorate the mask with glitter glue and markers as you wish.

#6

7. Glue a 6-inch piece of yarn to each side of the back of the mask near the eyeholes. Let the glue dry.

#7

8. Carefully place the mask over your face. Have an adult help you tie the yarn comfortably behind your head.

#8

MENORAH POP-UP CARD

Two hundred years B.C.E., the Jewish people of what is now Israel were ruled by a foreign king who did not respect their right to worship. The Jews rebelled against this king and drove his armies out of their land. To celebrate their victory, they wanted to light an oil lamp in their temple and let it shine forever, but they only had enough oil for one day. Miraculously, the lamp's flame glowed brightly for eight days! People honor this miracle on Hanukkah or Chanukah, which means "dedication," by lighting candles on a special candleholder called a menorah.

WHAT YOU WILL NEED:

- scissors
- white card stock paper
- pencil
- crayons, colored pencils, or markers
- ruler
- construction paper
- glue or paste

WHAT TO DO:

1. Print and cut out the menorah pattern from page 40. Use a pencil or marker to trace it onto the white card stock paper.

#1

#2

2. Color the candles and decorate the menorah with crayons or markers as you wish.

3. Cut along the solid lines of the pattern.

#3

4. Use a ruler and pencil to copy the pop-up card pattern to another sheet of card stock. Cut along the solid lines and fold along the dashed lines. On page 38, there is an explanation of how to fold the dashed lines.

#4

5. Fold the construction paper in half to form the outside of the card. Put a little glue or paste along the edges of the card stock and center it in place inside the construction paper.

#5

6. Glue or paste the menorah into place on the pop-up portion of the inside of the card. Let it dry.

7. Write a greeting on the outside or inside of the card.

Happy Hanukkah

8. If you wish, you can fold the paper flames down behind the candles on the pop-up menorah and raise them up each day of Hanukkah.

#8

Have a bright Holiday!

REINDEER MARIONETTE

The reindeer of northern Europe are also known as caribou in Alaska and northern Canada. They have large hooves that help them run in snow and ice. In the Arctic lands of northern Europe, ancient people trained these deer to pull sleighs and carry bundles. Reindeer are still used as work animals. No wonder Santa Claus uses these strong and nimble creatures to pull his sleigh through the snow!

WHAT YOU WILL NEED:

- air-drying clay
- a plastic stir stick or small straw
- a wooden toothpick
- pipe cleaners
- scissors
- craft foam

- acrylic or watercolor paints
- paintbrush
- yarn
- string or fishing line
- large craft sticks
- duct tape

What to do:

1. Sculpt a head, body, and four feet from the clay. While the clay is still soft, use the stir stick or straw to make two holes in the front and back of the body for the yarn to go through for the head and legs. Push a hole through the tops of all the feet and through the back of the head. Use the toothpick to make a small hole through the clay pieces for the control strings. Make small holes through the side of the head near the front of the ears and through the middle of the body near the top.

2. While the clay is still soft, stick small antlers made from pieces of pipe cleaner and craft foam ears into the head and a foam tail into the body. Let the clay dry.

#2

3. Paint the dry clay pieces with acrylic paints or watercolors as you wish. Let them dry.

#4

4. Use yarn to connect the different parts together. One piece of yarn can be used for the front feet and another piece for the back feet. One piece of yarn can loop through the front hole in the body to attach the head. Tie knots in the yarn to keep all the pieces in the right place.

5. Thread about 12 inches of string or fishing line through the small holes and tie them in place.

6. Use small pieces of duct tape to fasten the ends of the strings to the craft stick control bar. Hold the control bar up and adjust the length of the strings so that all the feet hang evenly and the head looks forward.

#6

7. Hold the puppet so that the feet rest lightly on a table top or puppet stage. Gently rock the control bar to make the legs move. Tilt the bar forward and back to make the head go up and down.

#7

FUN AND FESTIVE HOLIDAY HAT

Winter time is a season of parties and family gatherings! Christmas, Hanukkah, New Year's Eve, and Mardi Gras are all celebrated in the winter. Whichever holiday you want to celebrate, make it even more fun with a festive party hat!

WHAT YOU WILL NEED:

- ❄ scissors
- ❄ pencil
- ❄ crayons and markers
- ❄ plastic table covers or tissue paper—in assorted colors*
- ❄ glue stick
- ❄ poster board

- ❄ plastic jewels, glitter glue, crepe paper streamers, and cotton balls (optional)
- ❄ cellophane tape

*Author's note: Plastic table covers are lightweight and inexpensive and come in a wide variety of colors. They can be found at many department and craft stores in the party section.

WHAT TO DO:

1. Print and cut out the hat pattern from page 43. Use a pencil or marker to trace four patterns onto the plastic table covers or tissue paper in the colors you wish. For special holiday colors, see the note below. Cut the patterns out.

#1

2. Lay the triangle pattern pieces in front of you. Rub the glue stick along both the long edges of one triangle. Glue the long edges of two other triangle pattern pieces to each side of the first triangle pattern. Let them dry.

#2

Note: Holidays have certain colors that are often associated with them, which you may want to consider when you make your party hats: Christmas = red, white, and green, often with fluffy, white trim; Hanukkah = blue and white; Mardi Gras = green, gold, and purple.

3. Glue the last pattern piece to the other free edges. Let them dry. Do not put any glue on the bottom edges.

4. Cut the poster board to make a strip 2 inches by 24 inches.

5. Decorate one side of the poster board strip with crayons, markers, plastic jewels, glitter glue, crepe paper streamers, or cotton as you wish.

#3

#5

6. Have an adult help you gently bend the poster board strip into a circle that will comfortably fit your head. Use tape to fasten the ends together behind your head.

7. Use tape to fasten the bottom edge of your cone-shaped pattern piece around the inside of the poster board ring.

#7

Groundhog Pop-up Puppet

The groundhog is a large rodent that lives in a burrow. Early German settlers to the United States brought with them a tradition of forecasting the weather on February 2 based on the behaviors of burrowing animals. The tradition claims that if the groundhog pops out of his burrow on that day and sees his shadow, there will be six more weeks of winter. The people of Punxsutawney, Pennsylvania, make Groundhog Day a big celebration every year. Thousands of people watch Punxsutawney Phil, the official groundhog, predict the weather!

What you will need:

- a small cylindrical container (like an oatmeal container)
- scissors
- permanent markers
- brown fabric
- sewing needle and thread (with adult supervision)
- air-drying clay
- a 12-inch dowel, ¼ inch in diameter
- acrylic paint and paintbrush
- glue
- rickrack, fabric scraps, or cotton balls (optional)
- a large bead with a ¼-inch opening (optional)

WHAT TO DO:

1. Remove the top of the cylindrical container. Have an adult help you cut the top off with scissors. Make a small hole in the center of the bottom large enough for the dowel to slide through smoothly.

#1

2. Print and cut out the groundhog pattern from page 44. Use a marker to trace the pattern onto the fabric. Cut two copies of the pattern. Be sure that the pattern pieces will fit snuggly around the top of the container with a little extra to allow for sewing the pieces together.

#2

#3

3. With an adult's help, sew the pattern pieces together along the sides as shown. Do not sew the top or bottom flat edges. Once sewn together, turn the piece inside out so that the stitching and seams are hidden inside. (**Note:** If the fabric is furry on one side, be sure to sew it with the furry sides facing each other. You may use a thin line of glue to fasten the sides of the pattern pieces together rather than sewing them if you wish. Let them dry.)

4. Put a ball of clay, about the size of a walnut, on one end of the dowel and sculpt it to look like a groundhog's head. Let it dry.

5. Paint the groundhog's head and the cylinder as you wish. Let them dry.

#4

#5

6. Glue the wide bottom of the fabric body around the edge of the top of the cylinder. Insert the rod with the head into the body and glue the top of the body to the rod just under the puppet's head. Let the glue dry.

#8

7. Decorate the line where the puppet fabric meets the container with rickrack or cloth scraps or cotton balls. Add a bead to the bare end of the dowel if you wish.

8. Hold the bottom of the completed puppet in one hand and gently push and pull the bottom of the dowel with the other hand to make the groundhog pop in and out of his hole to see his shadow.

CHRISTMAS TREE MAGAZINE SCULPTURE

Martin Luther, a famous German religious leader, was impressed by the beauty of the stars sparkling through the branches of an evergreen tree on a cold winter night. He set up a little evergreen tree in his home at Christmas time and decorated it with little candles and shiny ornaments as symbols of ever-renewing life and light. German immigrants brought the tradition of the Christmas tree to the United States. Here is a little Christmas tree that you can use as a decoration for many winters to come.

WHAT YOU WILL NEED:

- two or three outdated magazines or catalogs of the same size (Get adult permission before using recycled materials.)
- glue
- poster or acrylic paint
- paintbrush
- plastic jewels
- glitter glue
- small ornaments, pipe cleaners, and cotton balls (optional)

WHAT TO DO:

1. Place a magazine or catalog in front of you with the back cover up.

2. Fold the top right corner of the back cover in until it meets the center. The top of the back page will now meet the center fold of the magazine. Crease the folded edge.

#2

#3

3. Fold the angled edge of the page into the center.

4. Fold each page of the magazine as you did in Steps 2 and 3. You will be amazed at how quickly you can do this!

#4

5. Repeat Steps 1 to 4 for the second magazine or catalog.

6. Stand the sculpted pieces up on their wide base and glue the outside pages together. Let them dry.

7. Spread out the pages of the tree sculpture to make it look even.

8. Paint the sculpture with poster or acrylic paint. Be sure that the paint is not too thin or runny. Let the paint dry.

#8

9. Decorate the tree sculpture by gluing plastic jewels, glitter glue, ornaments, pipe cleaner garlands, or cotton pieces as you wish.

#9

PATTERNS

The percentages included on the patterns tell you how much to enlarge or shrink the image using a copier. Most copiers and printers have an adjustable size/percentage feature to change the size of an image when you print it. After you print the pattern to its correct size, cut it out. Trace it onto the material listed in the craft.

*Instructions for folding the inside of the pop-up menorah card:

1. Fold the card stock in half along the long dashed line.

2. Cut along the two short solid lines. You now have a small flap in between the two lines.

3. Fold over the small flap along the short dashed line to create a crease. Put the flap back in place.

4. Open the card and gently push the flap through. It will be folded the opposite way to the rest of the card and look like a little bench.

Menorah Pop-up Card

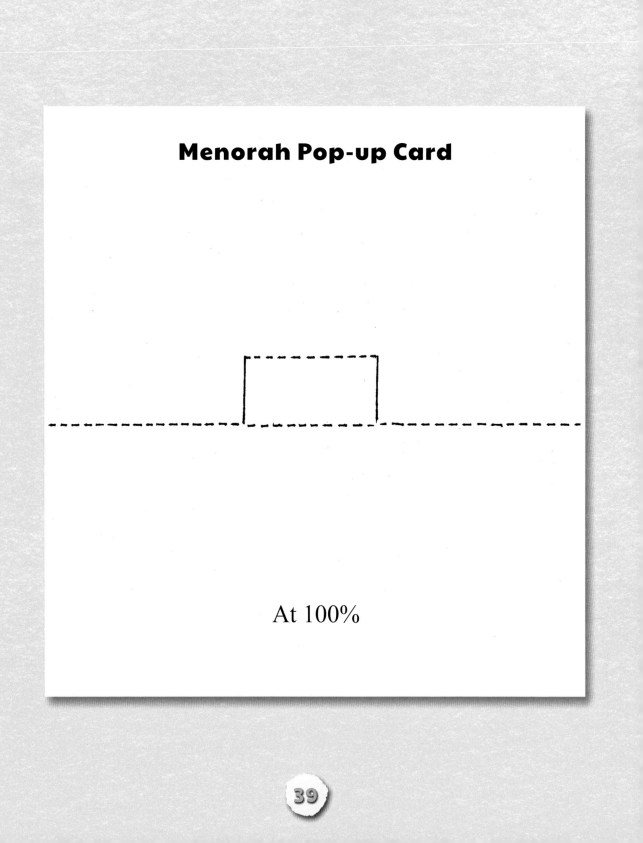

At 100%

Menorah Pop-up Card*

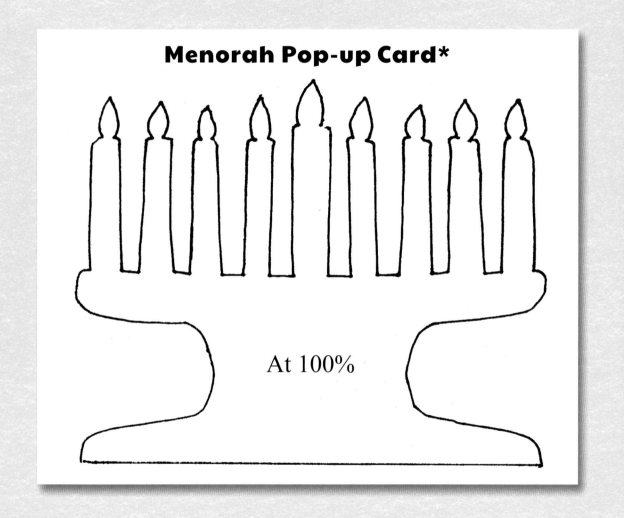

At 100%

1. Copy or scan the pattern for the mask.

2. Enlarge it to its correct size. It is a very big pattern, so you will need to print it out in two parts.

3. Tape the two parts together.

4. Cut along all the solid black lines and cut out the darkened area.

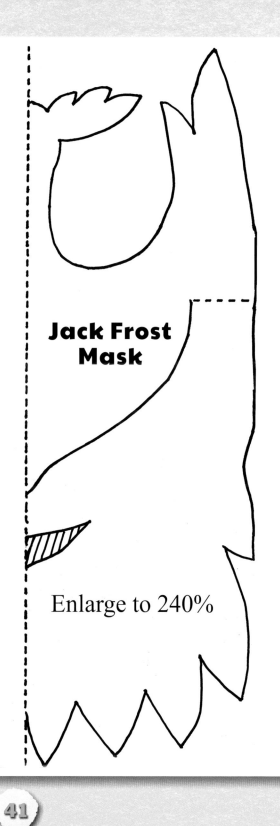

Jack Frost Mask

Enlarge to 240%

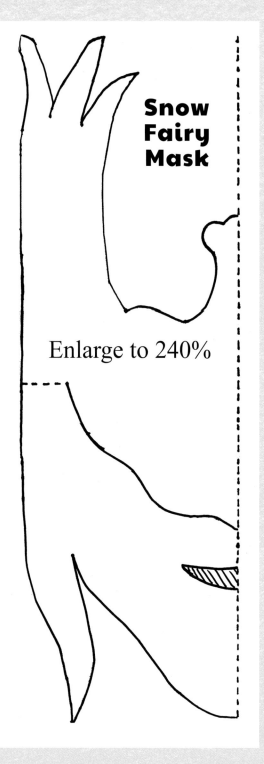

Snow Fairy Mask

Enlarge to 240%

Follow the same instructions on page 41.

Fun and Festive Holiday Hats

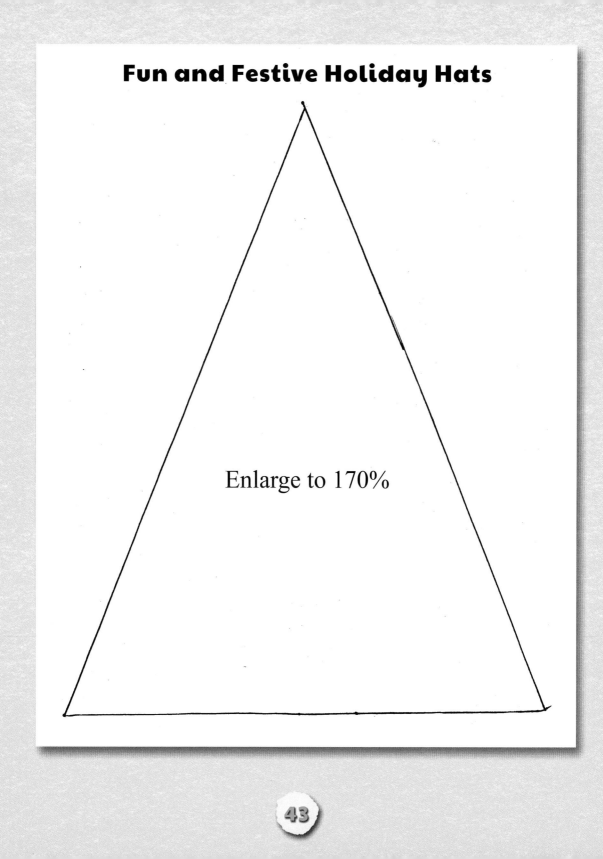

Enlarge to 170%

Groundhog Pop-up Puppet

DO NOT SEW HERE

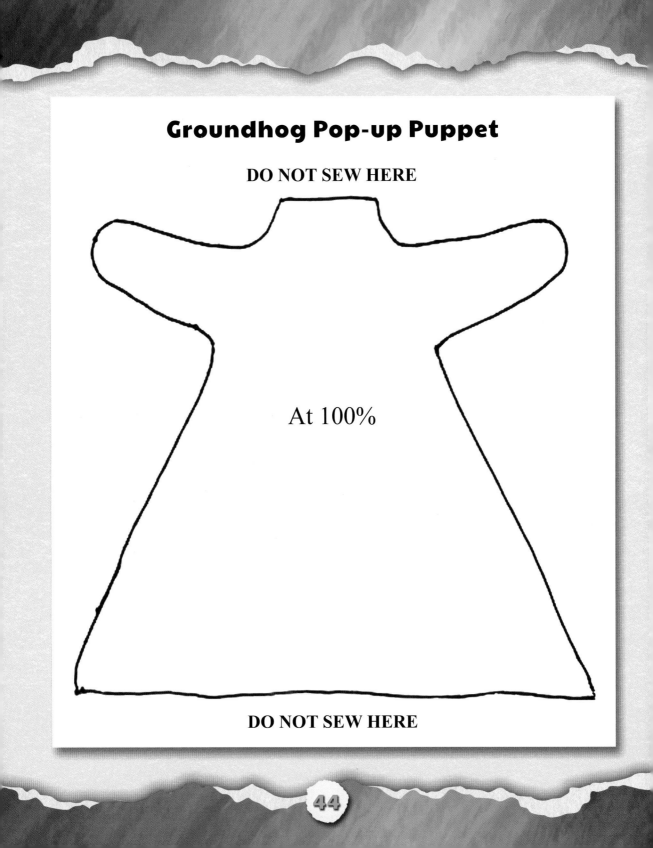

At 100%

DO NOT SEW HERE

READ ABOUT

Books

Castaldo, Nancy F. *Winter Day Play: Activities, Crafts, and Games for Indoors and Out.* Chicago: Chicago Review Press, 2008.

Rau, Dana Meachen. *Creating Winter Crafts.* North Mankato, Minn.: Cherry Lake Publishing, 2013.

Ross, Kathy. *Step-by-Step Crafts for Winter.* Honesdale, Penn.: Boyds Mills Press, 2006.

Internet Addresses

Spoonful: Winter Crafts

http://spoonful.com/winter/winter-crafts

DLTK's Crafts for Kids: Winter Crafts

http://www.dltk-holidays.com/winter/
crafts.html

Visit Randel McGee's Web site at
http://www.mcgeeproductions.com

INDEX

About the Author

Randel McGee has liked to make things and has played with paper and scissors as long as he can remember. He also likes telling stories and

performing. He is an internationally recognized storyteller, ventriloquist, and puppeteer. He and his dragon puppet, Groark, have performed all around the United States and Asia and have appeared in two award-winning video series on character education. He also portrays the famous author Hans Christian Andersen in storytelling performances, where he makes amazing cut-paper designs while he tells stories, just like Andersen did. He likes showing teachers and children the fun they can have with paper projects, storytelling, and puppetry. Randel McGee lives in central California with his wife, Marsha. They have five grown children.